D0208168

Cooking in the Nude

For Golf Lovers

Designed by Carolyn Weary Brandt
Edited by Natalie Gehl and Meghan Mitchell

©1998 by Debbie and Stephen Cornwell.
All rights reserved.
This book, or any portion thereof, may not be reproduced or transmitted in any form or
by any means, electronic or mechanical, including photocopying, recording, or by any
information storage and retrieval system, without permission in writing from
the copyright holders.

Library of Congress Catalog Card Number: 98-74029

Printed in Canada
Published by Howell Press, Inc., 1713-2D Allied Lane,
Charlottesville, VA 22903
Telephone: (434) 977-4006
www.howellpress.com

Fifth Printing 2003

HOWELL PRESS

TABLE OF CONTENTS

FORE!!!
(Introduction)

*C*ooking in the Nude for Golf Lovers is an irresistibly romantic collection of flirtatious recipes that is sure to spice up all of your post-game activities! It's for *golf lovers*, who *are* lovers! And while we won't guarantee it will lower your score on the course, it will certainly increase your chances of "scoring" well after the clubs are put away.

As one famous golfer said, "First you've got to be good, then you've got to be lucky!" If you want to get lucky, don't leave anything to chance. Before you take your most seductive shot with our "Shoot to Thrill" entrées, we encourage you to plan your game strategy well by reading the other chapters. Whether you want to indulge in a romantic romp or an elegant affair, there is an art to "Playing a Round" (creating the mood). Then, make sure you're really ready to find that "Fairway to Heaven" by reviewing our list of pantry needs. *Now* you're ready to learn "How to Swing" with an enticing presentation and suggestive ambiance.

Get the picture? Just as on the golf course, the best scores require some setup and strategy! Be ready to practice some serious "Fore Play" with an appetizer or two. Then invite your partner to play the "Fast Greens" (salads) before you win the match with your "Shoot to Thrill" entrée! We've even provided a "Scorecard" so you can take notes on what works best in this culinary game. So no matter what your handicap is on the course, you won't have any obstacles after dinner tonight!

PLAYING A ROUND
(Creating the Mood)

*Y*ou've just spent an exhilarating day on a beautiful seaside course with your favorite partner. Or, maybe the two of you have just returned from the Pro-Am, and you're still sharing the satisfaction of seeing celebrities make the same mistakes you do! Whether it's a wooded country club or a desert venue, whether you're the players or in the gallery, you love the game of golf!

Now you're driving home for the evening, and after spending a day pursuing your favorite sporting passion, you're thinking it's time for some other passion and a different kind of game! Yes, we're talking about seducing your sporting partner in a spirited game of culinary conquest!

Take advantage of the time during the drive home to get your lover's passion refocused on you. (If you live on the 7th fairway and you're walking home, you'd better start talking—fast!) But, for most of us, the golf course is probably a bit of a drive, and you can make good use of this opportunity to get your lover in the mood. Toward the end of the day, it's natural that the conversation might turn to food, and since eating is one of the most sensual shared pleasures on Earth, it's a natural progression from there to romantic repartee . . .

You might start by asking your companion if he or she knows the real meaning of the expression, "It's a Gimme." If you get the proper reaction, you might go on to suggest a little "Fore Play" (from our assortment of appetizers). As the conversation progresses you'll be amazed at how stimulating golfing terminology can be; from knickers and drivers to bounce and squeeze plays that wind up in the rough, you'll find whole new meanings! And as you finally arrive home,

you'll know you've created the right mood because your lover's libido is telling you . . . I'm Game If You Are. Find out how sporting your partner really is . . . right after dinner tonight!

HOW TO SWING
(Presentation)

*J*ust as knowing how to swing is a must for scoring at golf, presentation is the pièce de *no* résistance when it comes to romantic dining. Yet it needn't be pretentious. After a day on the course, a simple setting is best. A casual tablecloth, with a colorful floral arrangement and a little sparkling candlelight, will send a very strong message—in part because it probably won't be expected.

But *you* know how to swing! Before you left this morning, you took care of a few details: you left a good bottle of wine to chill and chose an assortment of CDs that you knew would have the desired effect on your lover's libido later that evening. You also made sure that the kids (if any) are staying over with friends tonight and that the phone is off the hook. (Yes, you're beginning to fantasize about golf as a contact sport!)

Because you anticipated this moment so well, you'll have no trouble at all making a fast transition from the 18th hole to the first course, and then, shall we say, to the final course. We guarantee that before the evening is through your partner will have no doubts about your ability to swing. This just may be the best round you've ever played . . . !

A FAIRWAY TO HEAVEN
(The Well-Stocked Pantry)

Allspice	Button mushrooms	Cumin
Almonds, whole, peeled	Cappellini pasta	Currants
Anchovy fillets	Carrots	Curry powder
Apple cider vinegar	Cauliflower	Dill, fresh
Apples	Cayenne pepper	Drambuie
Arugula	Celery	Dried apricots
Asiago cheese	Celery salt	Dried cranberries
Asparagus	Cherry tomatoes	Egg noodles
Avocados	Chervil	Feta cheese
Baking soda	Chèvre (goat) cheese	Fish stock
Balsamic vinegar	Chicken broth	Flour, all-purpose
Bananas	Chives, fresh	Frisée
Basil	Chutney, mango	Garbanzo beans, canned
Bay leaves	Cilantro	Garlic
Beef broth	Cinnamon sticks	Garlic salt
Black beans, canned	Clam juice, bottled	Ginger
Black olives	Coconut, shredded	Grand Marnier or
Blue cheese	Coconut milk, light	orange liqueur
Boboli pizza crust	Coriander	Green beans
Bourbon	Corn, canned	Green bell peppers
Bowtie pasta	Corn oil	Green leaf lettuce
Brandy	Cornmeal, yellow	Green onions
Bread crumbs	Cottage cheese, small curd	Gruyère cheese
Brown sugar	Crackers, unsalted	Honey
Burgundy	Cranberries	Horseradish
Butter	Cream cheese	Hot pepper sauce
Butter leaf lettuce	Crimini mushrooms	Jalapeño peppers
Butternut squash	Cucumbers	Kalamata olives

Kiwi
Leeks
Lemons/Lemon peel
Limes/Lime peel
Mace
Madeira
Marjoram
Mayonnaise
Milk
Mizuna
Molasses
Monterey Jack cheese
Mozzarella cheese
Mustard, Dijon
Mustard, dry
Mustard, yellow,
  prepared
Nutmeg
Olive oil, light
Orange juice concen-
  trate, frozen
Oranges/Orange peel
Oregano
Paprika
Parmesan cheese
Parsley
Peanuts
Pears (comice)
Peas, frozen
Penne pasta
Pepper
Pine nuts

Poppy seeds
Port
Portabello mushrooms
Potatoes, red, small
Poultry seasoning
Prosciutto
Radicchio
Raisins, cranberry
Raisins, golden
Red bell peppers
Red leaf lettuce
Red onion
Red wine vinegar
Rice vinegar
Rice, white
Rice, wild
Roma tomatoes
Romaine lettuce
Rosemary
Russet potatoes
Rutabagas
Saffron
Sage
Salmon, smoked
Salt
Salt cooking oil
Saltine cracker crumbs
Scotch whiskey
Sesame oil
Sesame seeds
Shallots
Sherry

Sour cream
Soy sauce, light
Spaghettini pasta
Spinach, fresh
Spinach, chopped,
  frozen
Sugar
Sun-dried tomatoes,
  in olive oil
Sweet potatoes
Swiss cheese
Tarragon
Tequila
Thyme
Tomato paste
Tomatoes, chopped
  and peeled, canned
Vegetable broth
Vegetable oil
Walnut oil
Walnut pieces
Wasa bread
Whipping cream
White beans, small,
  canned
White wine, dry (Sau-
  ternes, if available)
Worcestershire sauce
Yellow onions
Yogurt, plain
Zinfandel
Zucchini

Roasted Red Bell Pepper Spread   30 minutes

Step One:

1 cup mayonnaise
1/2 cup sour cream
1 7-oz. jar roasted red bell peppers
1 small clove garlic, minced

Pat moisture from peppers with paper towel. Combine ingredients in food processor; blend until smooth. Avoid overblending.

Step Two:

1 Tbsp. chives, minced

Fold chives into dip. Refrigerate up to 1 hour before serving. Serve with crackers or sliced baguette.

Chive and Salmon Spread   30 minutes

Step One:

8 oz. nonfat cream cheese, room
    temperature
1/4 cup whipping cream
1/2 tsp. fresh lemon juice
1 tsp. prepared horseradish
3-4 Tbsp. fresh snipped chives

In bowl, mix ingredients together.

Step Two:

4 oz. smoked salmon
1-2 parsley sprigs

Using two forks, shred salmon. Gently fold salmon into cream cheese. Spoon cheese into serving dish, garnish with parsley, and serve with unsalted crackers.

Corn, Basil, and Sun-Dried Tomato Cakes

25 minutes

Step One:
1/2 cup yellow cornmeal
2 Tbsp. flour
1/2 tsp. baking soda
1/2 tsp. salt
1/2 cup milk
3 sun-dried tomatoes in olive oil
2 Tbsp. minced fresh basil

Combine cornmeal, flour, baking soda, and salt; mix well. Whisk in milk. Chop tomatoes. Add tomatoes and basil to batter, stirring to blend.

Step Two:
3 Tbsp. cooking oil

Preheat broiler. Heat oil in large frying pan over medium heat until shimmering. Using a tablespoon, add batter to pan to make small pancakes. Fry until brown; turn and fry until brown. Remove and place on paper towels.

Step Three:
2 oz. shredded Monterey Jack cheese
2 Tbsp. minced fresh basil

Move pancakes to broiler pan and top each with small bit of cheese. Broil 5-6 inches from heat until melted. Sprinkle with basil and serve.

Feta Cheese Spread

25 minutes

Step One:
3 oz. feta cheese
8 oz. light cream cheese
1 Tbsp. sour cream
3 Tbsp. minced shallot
1 small clove garlic, minced
1/2 tsp. dill
1/4 tsp. oregano
1/4 tsp. chervil
1/4 tsp. marjoram
1 Tbsp. minced fresh parsley
1/2 cup chopped black olives

Blend feta cheese, cream cheese, and sour cream together. Add remaining ingredients, except olives, and blend well. Fold in olives. Spoon into serving bowl or crock; cover and chill. Serve with broken wasa bread or unsalted crackers.

Crab Caps

45 minutes

Step One:

6-8 large fresh mushrooms, stems removed and reserved

olive oil

Turn washed caps upside down on baking sheet and brush lightly with oil. Turn caps over, cavity side up.

Step Two:

reserved mushroom stems, minced
1 1/2 Tbsp. butter
3 Tbsp. minced onion
4 tsp. flour
1/4 cup fresh crabmeat
2 tsp. dry sherry
2 tsp. fresh minced parsley
salt and pepper to taste
4 Tbsp. grated Gruyère cheese

Melt butter in frying pan over medium heat. Add onion and sauté 5 minutes. Whisk in flour and add all remaining ingredients except cheese. Sauté 2-3 minutes, until heated through. Stuff caps and sprinkle with cheese. Bake at 375°F for 15 minutes.

Hot Crab Morsels

30 minutes

Step One:

1/2 lb. crabmeat
1/3 cup saltine cracker crumbs
1 large egg, beaten
2 tsp. minced shallot or onion
1 Tbsp. mayonnaise
1 tsp. Worcestershire sauce
1 tsp. prepared mustard
1/8-1/4 tsp. hot pepper sauce

Squeeze extra moisture from crabmeat. Blend all ingredients well and roll into bite-size balls. Place on sheet of waxed paper. You may cover and refrigerate until ready to use.

Step Two:

fine saltine cracker crumbs
oil

Roll balls in cracker crumbs to coat; return to waxed paper. Heat oil in frying pan until almost smoking. Add several balls at a time, frying on all sides until golden. Place on paper towels to drain.

Step Three:

parsley sprigs
lemon wedges
fresh crab legs (optional)

Arrange crab balls on serving tray. Garnish with parsley, lemon wedges, and crab legs. Serve immediately.

Fast Greens

15 minutes

Zesty Dijon and Romaine Salad

Step One:

2 Tbsp. red wine vinegar
1 tsp. Dijon mustard
1/2 tsp. thyme
1/4 tsp. freshly ground pepper
3 flat anchovy fillets, mashed
6 Tbsp. light olive oil

Whisk all ingredients in bowl until well blended.

Step Two:

1 small head romaine lettuce
3 Tbsp. freshly grated Parmesan
   or Asiago cheese

Toss lettuce and dressing in bowl. Divide onto chilled salad plates. Sprinkle with cheese and serve.

Greens with Envy

15 minutes

Walnut, Pear, and Blue Cheese Salad

Step One:

2 tsp. fresh lemon juice
2 Tbsp. walnut oil
1/8 tsp. freshly ground pepper

Combine all ingredients in bottle with tight-fitting lid; shake until well blended.

Step Two:

1/2-3/4 lb. mixed greens (butter leaf,
   radicchio, frisée, arugula, romaine)
1 ripe pear, Comice or Bosc
1/2 cup walnut pieces
1/2 cup crumbled blue cheese

Tear greens into bite-size pieces and put into large salad bowl. Peel pears and cut into bite-size pieces. Add to greens. Sprinkle walnuts and cheese over mix; then add dressing and toss gently.

Orange You a Tee-s Salad

Orange, Avocado, and Pine Nut Salad

Step One:

2 cups fresh basil leaves, finely chopped
1/4 cup light olive oil
2 Tbsp. fresh orange juice

Put basil, olive oil, and juice in blender or food processor. Process just long enough to mix oil with leaves; do not puree.

Step Two:

1/4 cup pine nuts

In separate frying pan, toast nuts until lightly browned. Set aside 2 Tbsp. nuts. Coarsley chop the rest and add to dressing.

Step Three:

3 navel oranges, peeled and sliced
2 avocados, peeled and sliced

Alternate orange and avocado slices on salad plate. Drizzle with dressing. Sprinkle with unchopped nuts and serve.

♥ Playful Partners

45 minutes

As Jack Benny once said, "Give me good clubs, fresh air, and a beautiful partner . . . and you can keep the clubs and fresh air!"

Beef with Chèvre in Red Wine Sauce

Step One:

2 Tbsp. butter	Melt butter in frying pan. Sauté mushrooms
5-6 Crimini mushrooms	until tender. Place in a bowl. Add beef and
1 lb. lean ground beef	herbs, blending well. Shape into 4 patties.
1/2 tsp. thyme	
1/2 tsp. rosemary	
1/4 tsp. sage	

Step Two:

2 Tbsp. butter	Melt butter in frying pan over medium heat.
salt	Add patties and season well with salt and
freshly ground pepper	pepper. Cook until brown (about 5 minutes);
4 thick slices chèvre cheese	turn patties over. Season with salt and pepper.
1/2 tsp. thyme	Lay a slice of cheese atop each patty and
1/2 tsp. rosemary	sprinkle with herbs. Continue cooking 3-5
1/2 tsp. sage	minutes, to desired doneness. Transfer to warm
	plates.

Step Three:

1 Tbsp. butter	Add butter to pan. Sauté shallots until soft and
1 shallot, minced	translucent. Add wine. Bring to a boil,
1/2 cup burgundy	whisking bits from bottom of pan, and boil
3 Tbsp. minced parsley	until sauce is reduced to about 1/4 cup and is
	slightly syrupy. Spoon sauce over patties,
	garnish with parsley, and serve.

SUGGESTED MENU

"Fore" Play

Corn, Basil, and Sun-Dried Tomato Cakes

Fast Greens

Zesty Dijon and Romaine Salad

Shoot to Thrill

Playful Partners

It's a Gimme

Red Potatoes with Chive and Pepper Butter

Wine

Pinot Noir

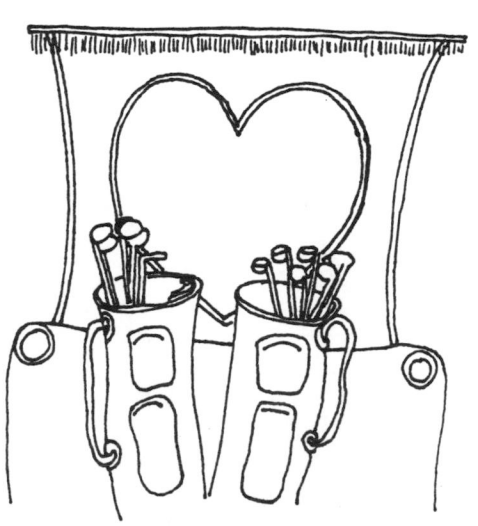

Par for the Course 2 hours

Every play for you is a pièce de no résistance, and your score . . . always par excellence!

Coconut Curried Beef

Step One:

2 Tbsp. olive oil
1 lb. lean stew meat, cut into 1" cubes
1 onion, chopped
1 tsp. curry powder
2/3 cup water
1/3 cup light coconut milk
1 tsp. allspice
1/2 tsp. salt
pinch cayenne pepper

Add oil to frying pan over medium heat; brown beef on all sides. Move beef to bowl. Add onion to pan and sauté until soft. Push onions aside; add curry and cook 15 seconds. Add remaining ingredients and bring to a boil over high heat. Return beef to pan; cover and simmer 1 1/2 hours over low heat.

Step Two:

2 carrots, cut into 1" pieces
1 apple, diced
1/3 cup dried apricots, diced
1 Tbsp. fresh lime juice
hot cooked rice
condiments:
   chopped salted peanuts
   shredded coconut
   raisins
   chutney

Add carrots, apple, and apricots to pan. Cover and continue cooking until almost tender, about 15 minutes. Stir in lime juice and continue cooking until vegetables are done. Serve on a bed of rice with condiments.

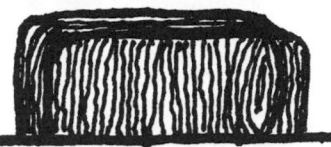

SUGGESTED MENU

"Fore" Play

Crab Caps

Fast Greens

*Walnut, Pear, and
Blue Cheese Salad*

Shoot to Thrill

♥Par for the Course

It's a Gimme

Swiss Cauliflower

Wine

Pinot Noir

 # Tees Me

. . . 'cause I love a big tease!

Braised Veal Shanks in Rich Vegetable Herb Sauce

Step One:

2 Tbsp. butter
2 Tbsp. olive oil
2 lb. veal shanks
1/2 cup flour

Melt butter and oil in large flameproof casserole dish. Put flour in plastic bag; add veal and shake to coat. Sauté veal on all sides until brown. Transfer to medium-size bowl.

Step Two:

2 onions, chopped
3 cloves garlic, minced
1 rib celery, chopped
1 carrot, chopped

Add onions, garlic, carrots, and celery to pan. Sauté until tender. Add veal to pan, atop vegetables. Make sure the bones are upright.

Step Three:

1/2 tsp. each marjoram, basil, thyme
1 tsp. poultry seasoning
2 15-oz. cans diced tomatoes
2 Tbsp. tomato paste
2 cups dry white wine
1 cup chicken broth
1/2 cup chopped parsley
grated peel of one lemon
1 bay leaf

Sprinkle herbs over veal. Add remaining ingredients. Bring to a boil; reduce heat to low, cover, and continue to cook 2 hours, or until veal is tender. Transfer veal to heated plates; cover and keep warm. Bring sauce to a boil and reduce amount by half (approximately 15 minutes). Ladle sauce over veal and serve.

SUGGESTED MENU

"Fore" Play
Chive and Salmon Spread

Fast Greens
Walnut, Pear, and Blue Cheese Salad

Shoot to Thrill
Tees Me

It's a Gimme
Red Potatoes with Chive and Pepper Butter

Wine
Cabernet Sauvignon

# Knickers Snickers

**3 hours, 45 minutes**

As Chi Chi Rodriguez once quipped, "Golf is the most fun you can have without taking your clothes off."

Spicy Caribbean Beef Stew

Step One:

1/4 cup olive oil
2 lb. short ribs, trimmed
1/2 cup flour
1 tsp. salt
1 tsp. pepper

Combine flour, salt, and pepper in plastic bag; add beef and shake to coat. Heat oil in Dutch oven over medium heat; add beef and brown on all sides. Move beef to a bowl. Pour off all but 2 Tbsp. oil.

Step Two:

2 jalapeño peppers
3 cloves garlic, minced
1 rib celery, finely chopped
1 onion, chopped
1 bell pepper, chopped

Split peppers, seed, and roast over open flame or in broiler until charred. Place in paper bag and fold top tightly; steam 10 minutes. Add remaining vegetables to pan and sauté until soft. Scrape charred area off peppers; finely chop and add to pan.

Step Three:

2 Tbsp. brown sugar
2 Tbsp. red wine vinegar
2 tsp. Worcestershire sauce
1 1/2 tsp. thyme
2 bay leaves
1 1/2 tsp. paprika
1 can diced tomatoes

Stir remaining ingredients into pan and cook 10 minutes on medium heat. Return beef to pan and cover. Cook 3 hours on low heat.

Step Four:

3 cups hot cooked rice
2 sprigs parsley or cilantro

Mound rice on side of warmed plate; ladle stew next to rice. Garnish with parsley.

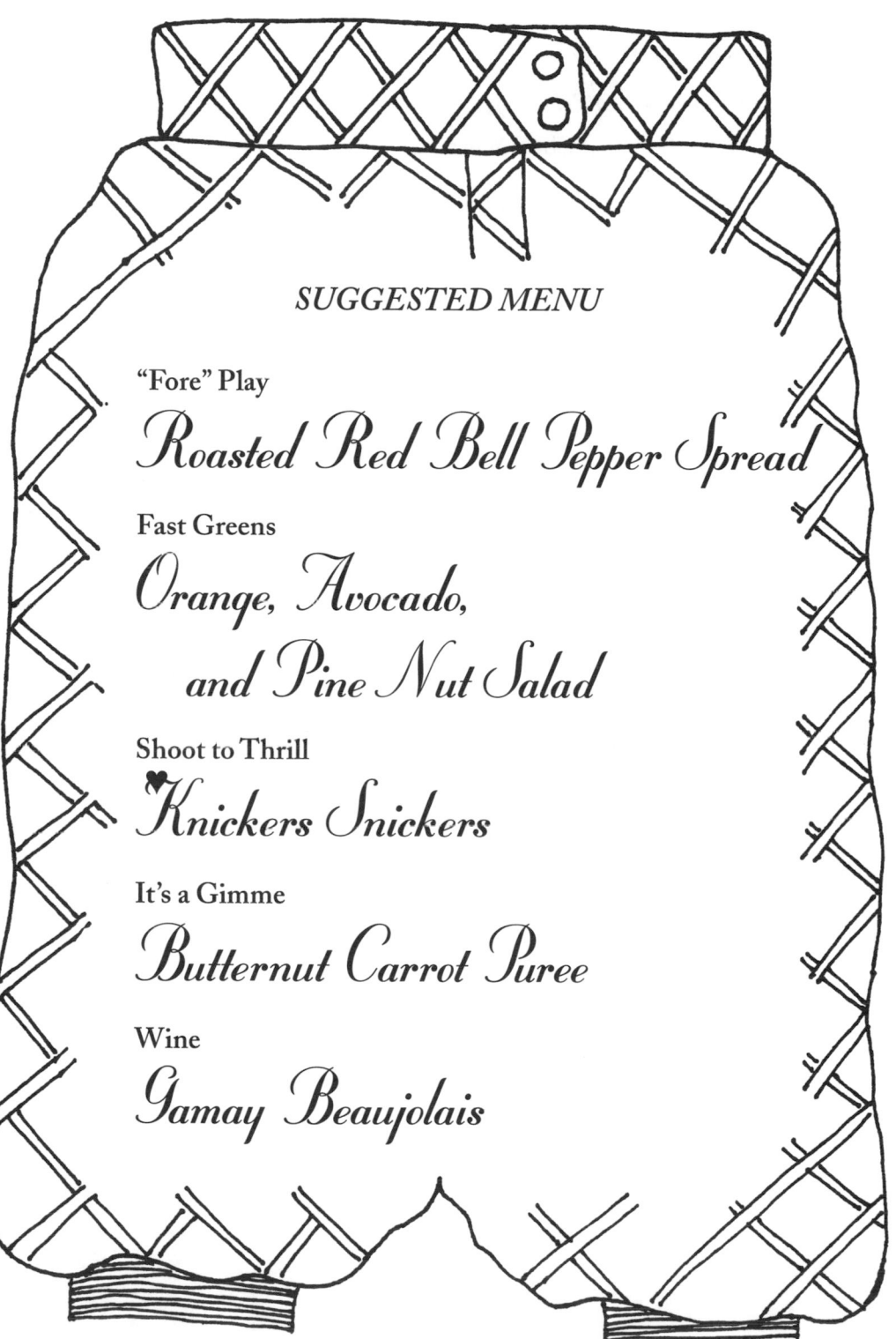

SUGGESTED MENU

"Fore" Play

Roasted Red Bell Pepper Spread

Fast Greens

Orange, Avocado,
and Pine Nut Salad

Shoot to Thrill

Knickers Snickers

It's a Gimme

Butternut Carrot Puree

Wine

Gamay Beaujolais

♥On the Green

. . . or in the trees, when no one's looking, I'll steal a squeeze!

Lime and Tequila Marinated Chicken with Guacamole

Step One:

1 jalapeño pepper, halved and seeded

Roast pepper over open flame or under broiler until charred. Place in paper bag and fold top tightly; steam 10 minutes. Scrape off charred bits, then mince and put in bowl.

Step Two:

4 tsp. tequila
1 Tbsp. corn oil
1 Tbsp. fresh lime juice
2 tsp. minced fresh cilantro
1 tsp. grated lime peel
1 tsp. honey
1/4 tsp. salt
freshly ground pepper
1 chicken breast, skinned and split

Combine all ingredients except chicken in bowl with jalapeños. Mix well. Add chicken and marinate 3-4 hours.

Step Three:

1 large avocado
1 Tbsp. fresh lemon juice
1/2 tsp. garlic salt
1/2-1 tsp. hot pepper sauce to taste

Preheat grill. Peel and seed avocado; then mash, using fork, in bowl. Blend in remaining ingredients. Remove chicken from marinade and grill until cooked through and springy to touch. Place chicken on warmed plates with a dollop of guacamole. Serve with hot cooked rice.

SUGGESTED MENU

"Fore" Play

Corn, Basil, and Sun-Dried Tomato Cakes

Fast Greens

Orange, Avocado, and Pine Nut Salad

Shoot to Thrill

♥On the Green

It's a Gimme

Butternut Carrot Puree

Wine

Sauvignon Blanc

♥ It's a Bounce and Squeeze Course

Wanna play a round?   **1 hour, 15 minutes**

Prosciutto- and Spinach-Stuffed Chicken Breasts

Step One:
3 Tbsp. butter
1 small onion, minced
1 large carrot, minced
8 large mushrooms, minced
salt and pepper to taste

Preheat oven to 375°F. Melt butter in frying pan over medium heat. Add onion and sauté until tender. Add carrots and mushrooms; continue to sauté until most of the moisture from the mushrooms has evaporated. Add seasonings.

Step Two:
4 large spinach leaves

Dip spinach leaves in boiling water until barely limp. Place on paper towel to drain.

Step Three:
1 lb. chicken breasts, skinned, boned, and pounded to 3/8" thickness
2 thin slices prosciutto or other smoked ham

Lay 1 slice ham over each breast. Lay 1-2 spinach leaves over ham. Spread 2 Tbsp. mushroom mixture over spinach. Roll breasts up, secure with toothpicks. Cover with wax paper and refrigerate 30 minutes. Remove toothpicks.

Step Four:
3 Tbsp. flour
salt and pepper to taste
1 1/2 Tbsp. oil

Mix flour, salt, and pepper on plate. Flour chicken lightly. Heat oil in frying pan over medium heat. Add breasts, seam side down, and brown on all sides; then transfer to baking dish and bake at 375°F for 6-8 minutes.

Step Five:
1 Tbsp. light olive oil
1 Tbsp. butter
1 cup minced mushrooms
1 clove garlic, minced
1 Tbsp. minced onion
1/2 cup whipping cream
1 Tbsp. dry sherry
2 tsp. snipped chives

Heat oil and butter in frying pan over medium heat. Sauté mushrooms, garlic, and onion until limp; most of the moisture will have evaporated. Add cream and sherry; increase heat and whisk sauce until thickened. Spoon over chicken and sprinkle with chives. Serve.

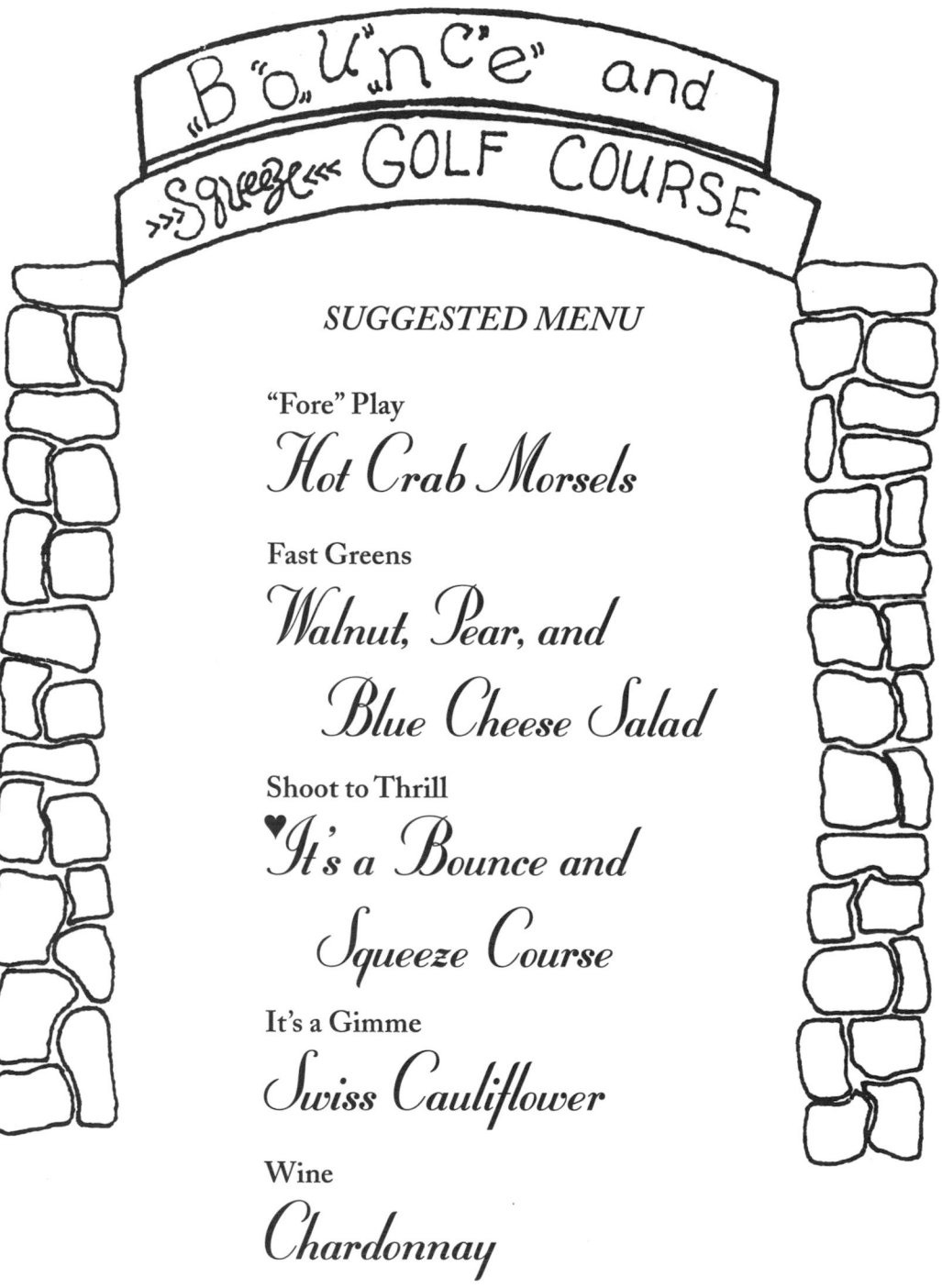

"Bounce" and "Squeeze" GOLF COURSE

SUGGESTED MENU

"Fore" Play
Hot Crab Morsels

Fast Greens
Walnut, Pear, and Blue Cheese Salad

Shoot to Thrill
♥It's a Bounce and Squeeze Course

It's a Gimme
Swiss Cauliflower

Wine
Chardonnay

♥Double Bogey Chicken

1 hour, 15 minutes

Sometimes extra strokes can be fun!

Island Chicken with Jump-Up Rice

Step One:
1 Tbsp. oil
1 green bell pepper, chopped
1 onion, chopped
1/3 lb. mushrooms, sliced
1 jalapeño pepper, seeded, minced
1 whole chicken breast, skinned, boned,
   cut into bite-size pieces

In large pot over medium heat, cook vegetables in oil until soft; move to bowl. Add chicken to pot and sauté 2-3 minutes. Return vegetables to pot.

Step Two:
2 cups chicken stock
4-6 Roma tomatoes, chopped
2 large carrots, peeled, chopped
1 potato, peeled, chopped
2 Tbsp. chopped fresh parsley
1 tsp. oregano
1/2-3/4 tsp. freshly ground pepper
1/2 tsp. salt
1 large ripe banana, chopped

Add all ingredients except banana to pot and turn heat up until liquid is just beginning to boil. Turn heat to medium-low and simmer until carrots and potatoes are tender, about 20 minutes. Add banana, stirring gently, and heat through.

Step Three:
1 Tbsp. oil
1 red bell pepper, finely chopped
1 onion, finely chopped
2 cloves garlic, minced
1/2 jalapeño pepper, seeded, minced
1 1/2 cups rice
2 1/2 cups water
1/2 cup light coconut milk
1 can black beans, rinsed
1 1/2 tsp. curry
1/2 tsp. thyme
freshly ground pepper
salt to taste

Meanwhile, in saucepan over medium heat, cook vegetables until soft. Add remaining ingredients, stirring well. Turn heat up. When mixture begins to boil, stir and reduce heat. Cover and cook until rice is done. Fluff rice and spoon onto warm plates; top with chicken. Garnish with a sprig of parsley and serve.

SUGGESTED MENU

"Fore" Play

Hot Crab Morsels

Fast Greens

Orange, Avocado, and Pine Nut Salad

Shoot to Thrill

Double Bogey Chicken

It's a Gimme

Butternut Carrot Puree

Wine

Gewürztraminer

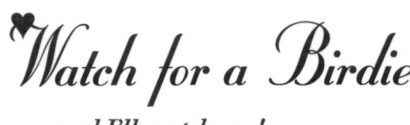# *Watch for a Birdie*

. . . and I'll watch you!

Ginger, Orange, and Sesame Chicken

Step One:

2 Tbsp. sesame seeds
1/2 cup fresh orange juice
1/4 cup fresh lemon juice
2 Tbsp. mango chutney
2 Tbsp. minced, peeled fresh ginger
1 1/2 Tbsp. grated orange peel
1 1/2 Tbsp. rice vinegar
2 tsp. sesame oil
1/8 tsp. cayenne pepper
1 chicken breast, skinned and split

Toast sesame seeds in dry frying pan until golden. Move seeds to dish. Whisk remaining ingredients except chicken into flat baking dish. Add chicken to dish, turning to coat. Marinate 1-2 hours.

Step Two:

3 Tbsp. butter
2 cups hot cooked rice
1 orange, cut into 1/4" slices

Remove chicken from marinade and roll in sesame seeds. Sauté in butter until golden, about 3-5 minutes per side. Move to warm plates. Mound rice next to chicken and garnish with orange slices.

SUGGESTED MENU

"Fore" Play

Roasted Red Bell Pepper Spread

Fast Greens

Walnut, Pear, and Blue Cheese Salad

Shoot to Thrill

Watch for a Birdie

It's a Gimme

French Kissed Peas

Wine

Chenin Blanc

You're Trapped!

I'm chipping away at your resistance.

Grilled Chicken with Corn and Dill Beurre Blanc

Step One:

1 cup finely chopped green onions
1 cup dry white wine
1/2 cup whipping cream
1/4 cup butter

In small saucepan over medium heat, bring onions and wine to a boil and simmer until only about 2 Tbsp. liquid remains. Add cream and continue to cook until it is reduced by half. Cut butter into small bits and whisk, bit by bit, into pan.

Step Two:

1 tsp. minced fresh dill
1/2 cup canned corn, drained
1 Roma tomato, finely chopped
salt and freshly ground pepper to taste

Preheat grill. Add remaining ingredients to saucepan; stir. Keep sauce warm.

Step Three:

1 chicken breast, skinned and split
oil

Brush chicken with oil and grill 3-5 minutes per side, until just done and springy to touch. Move to warm plates. Spoon sauce over chicken and serve.

SUGGESTED MENU

"Fore" Play
Chive and Salmon Spread

Fast Greens
Orange, Avocado, and Pine Nut Salad

Shoot to Thrill
You're Trapped

It's a Gimme
Red Potatoes with Chive and Pepper Butter

Wine
Chenin Blanc

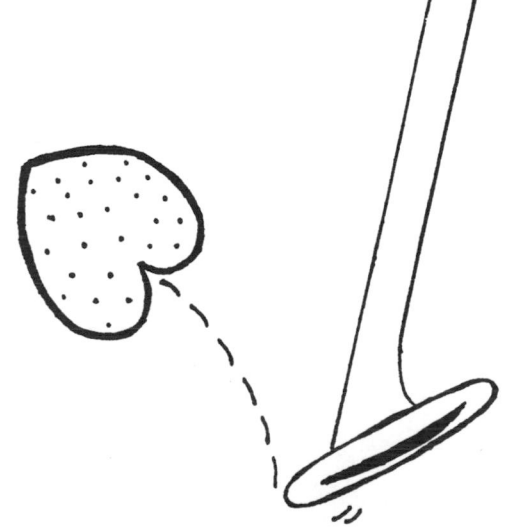

The Grass Is Always Greener

. . . on the course of true love!

Butternut Cranberry Salad with Grilled Chicken

Step One:

1/2 Tbsp. minced fresh ginger
1/4 tsp. salt
1 Tbsp. fresh lemon juice
1 Tbsp. apple cider vinegar
1/4 cup corn oil

Combine all ingredients in small jar and shake to blend well.

Step Two:

1 chicken breast, skinned and trimmed
of fat
oil

Brush chicken with oil and grill or broil until just done (springy to the touch). Let cool, then cut into 2" x 1/4" strips. Move to a medium-size bowl.

Step Three:

1 small butternut squash, peeled

Cut squash in half and remove seeds. Cut into 2" chunks, then into julienne strips about 1/8" wide. Put squash in boiling salted water. Return to a boil; drain in colander and rinse with cold water. Drain.

Step Four:

1/2 cup dried cranberries
1/2 lb. mixed greens (e.g., butter leaf,
romaine, red leaf, frisée, mizuna)

Add cranberries and squash to bowl with chicken. Gently toss with half the dressing. In separate bowl, toss greens with remaining dressing. Divide greens onto plates and arrange chicken mixture on top. Serve.

SUGGESTED MENU

"Fore" Play

Crab Caps

Shoot to Thrill

The Grass Is Always Greener

It's a Gimme

Sautéed Mushrooms with Madeira and Pine Nuts

Wine

Sauvignon Blanc

Put a Little Wiggle in Your Waggle

Braised Chicken Thighs with White Beans and Greens

Step One:

2 Tbsp. vegetable oil
2 Tbsp. flour
1/2 tsp. paprika
4-6 chicken thighs, skinned

Heat oil in frying pan over medium heat. Put flour and paprika in plastic bag; add chicken and shake to coat. In oil, brown chicken on all sides. Transfer to plate and keep warm.

Step Two:

3 Tbsp. tomato paste
1 1/4 cups chicken broth
1 onion, finely chopped
2 cloves garlic, minced
1 tsp. thyme
1/8 tsp. cayenne pepper
salt and pepper to taste

In small bowl, blend tomato paste and broth; set aside. Sauté onion and garlic in frying pan until soft. Return chicken to pan. Sprinkle with seasonings and pour broth over all.

Step Three:

1 16-oz. can small white beans
1 10-oz. pkg. frozen chopped spinach

Spoon beans over chicken. Spoon spinach over beans. Cover and cook over low heat for 35 minutes. Serve on warm plates.

SUGGESTED MENU

"Fore" Play

Crab Caps

Fast Greens

Orange, Avocado, and Pine Nut Salad

Shoot to Thrill

Put a Little Wiggle in Your Waggle

It's a Gimme

Butternut Carrot Puree

Wine

Chardonnay

♥ I'm Game If You Are

Find out how sporting your partner really is . . . after dinner!

Game Hens with Wild Rice and Fruit Stuffing

Step One:

1/4 cup wild rice
1 1/2 cups water

Bring rice and water to boil in small saucepan. Cover. Turn heat to low and simmer 45 minutes, or until tender.

Step Two:

1/2 cup white rice
1/2 tsp. salt
1 1/4 cups water

Bring water to boil. Add rice and salt; stir. Return to boil. Stir; turn heat to low and simmer until done, about 15 minutes.

Step Three:

2 Tbsp. butter
1 stalk celery, finely chopped
1/2 small onion, minced
4-5 Crimini or white mushrooms, finely chopped
1 tsp. poultry seasoning
salt and pepper to taste
1/3 cup mixed dried fruit, diced
(or 2 Tbsp. golden raisins, 2 Tbsp. cranberry raisins, and 1 Tbsp. currants)

Preheat oven to 350°F. Melt butter in frying pan over medium heat. Sauté onion, celery, and mushrooms until soft. Add seasonings. Stir in fruit and continue cooking until it begins to soften. Drain wild rice and add to pan. Add white rice to pan. Stir until well blended.

Step Four:

2 Cornish game hens, rinsed
salt and pepper to taste
2 Tbsp. fresh lemon juice
2 Tbsp. chopped parsley
4 Tbsp. butter

Salt and pepper hens inside and out. Spoon stuffing into hens and put in baking dish. Melt butter in small pan; add lemon juice and parsley. Brush hens with butter and bake 1 hour and 15 minutes. Baste occasionally with pan drippings.

SUGGESTED MENU

"Fore" Play

Chive and Salmon Spread

Fast Greens

Walnut, Pear, and Blue Cheese Salad

Shoot to Thrill

♥I'm Game If You Are

It's a Gimme

Green Beans with Prosciutto and Parmesan

Wine

Riesling

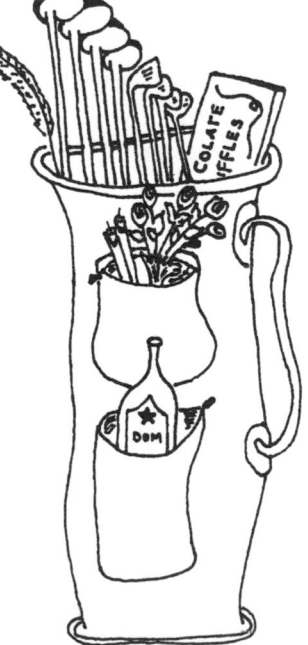

Putt Your Heart into It

"Love and putting are mysteries for the philosopher to resolve. Both are beyond golfers!" quipped Tommy Archer. Here's your chance to prove him wrong!

Ahi in Red Pepper Curry Sauce

Step One:

1/4 cup light olive oil
2 Tbsp. fresh lime juice
1 Tbsp. fresh lemon juice
1/2 tsp. cayenne pepper
1 lb. of Ahi steak

Combine marinade ingredients in flat dish, blending well. Add Ahi, turning to coat. Marinate 20 minutes.

Step Two:

1 jalapeño pepper
1 green bell pepper
1 red bell pepper
4 Tbsp. butter
3 cloves garlic, minced
1/2 onion, finely chopped

Halve, seed, and roast peppers over open flame or under broiler until charred. Transfer to paper bag and fold top tightly; steam for 10 minutes. Scrape charred bits off peppers and finely chop. In frying pan over medium heat, melt butter and sauté vegetables until softened.

Step Three:

1/2 cup grated fresh coconut
1 cup milk
1 1/2 Tbsp. fresh lime juice
2 tsp. curry powder

Add all ingredients to frying pan and simmer 5 minutes. In small batches, puree sauce in food processor. Return to pan and simmer until sauce is thick enough to coat the back of a spoon.

Step Four:

Preheat grill. Grill steaks until just done. Move to warm plates and spoon sauce over Ahi. Serve.

SUGGESTED MENU

"Fore" Play

Feta Cheese Spread

Fast Greens

Orange, Avocado, and Pine Nut Salad

Shoot to Thrill

Putt Your Heart into It

It's a Gimme

Green Beans with Prosciutto and Parmesan

Wine

Gewürztraminer

Tee for Two

45 minutes

. . . the course of the evening is up to you.

Prawns and Asparagus Tips in Grand Marnier Sauce

Step One:

1 large piece fresh ginger
2/3 cup water

Peel ginger and cut into matchsticks until you have about 1/4 cup. Pour water into small saucepan, add ginger and bring to a boil. Turn heat to low and simmer 10 minutes. Remove ginger; reserve 3 Tbsp. water.

Step Two:

2 Tbsp. butter
2 Tbsp. minced onion
1 lb. shrimp, shelled and deveined
1/2 tsp. rosemary, crushed
1/4 tsp. thyme
3 Tbsp. bourbon
1 Tbsp. Grand Marnier, or other
   orange liqueur
1/2 cup fish stock
1/3 cup whipping cream

Melt butter in frying pan over medium heat. Sauté onion until soft. Turn heat to high and add shrimp and herbs; sauté shrimp until just pink and move to a bowl. Add bourbon and Grand Marnier to frying pan and whisk constantly for one minute. Add reserved ginger water and fish stock. Boil until liquid is reduced to 1/4 cup. Add cream and boil until reduced by half. Return ginger and shrimp and juices to pan. Heat through.

Step Three:

1/3 lb. asparagus tips

Steam asparagus tips until crisp-tender. Fan tips out on warm plate. Ladle shrimp mixture at base of fan. Serve immediately.

SUGGESTED MENU

"Fore" Play

Hot Crab Morsels

Fast Greens

Walnut, Pear, and Blue Cheese Salad

Shoot to Thrill

Tee for Two

It's a Gimme

French Kissed Peas

Wine

Chenin Blanc

♥ Never Up, Never In

Putting is such sweet sorrow!

Snapper in Madeira Cream Sauce

Step One:
1 shallot, finely chopped
1 lb. snapper fillet
salt and pepper to taste
2/3 cup dry white wine (Sauternes,
  if available)
2/3 cup vegetable or chicken
  broth

Preheat oven to 400°F. Butter a large flame-proof baking dish and sprinkle bottom with shallot. Arrange snapper in single layer over shallot and season with salt and pepper. Add wine and broth. Place dish over medium heat and bring to a boil. Cover with foil and bake 10-15 minutes, or until snapper loses its translucency. Move snapper to warm plate; cover loosely and keep warm.

Step Two:
2/3 cup whipping cream
salt and pepper to taste

Place baking dish over high heat and boil until only 1/2 cup liquid remains, about 5 minutes. Reduce heat to medium and add cream, cooking until sauce coats back of spoon. Add salt and pepper.

Step Three:
1/2 cup finely chopped carrot
1/2 cup finely chopped celery
1/2 cup finely chopped shallot
2 Tbsp. brandy
2 Tbsp. Madeira
2 Tbsp. port

Combine all ingredients in a small saucepan and cook over high heat until liquid is evaporated. Blend vegetables into cream sauce; spoon over fish and serve.

SUGGESTED MENU

"Fore" Play

Roasted Red Bell Pepper Spread

Fast Greens

Walnut, Pear, and Blue Cheese Salad

Shoot to Thrill

♥*Never Up, Never In*

It's a Gimme

Swiss Cauliflower

Wine

Sauvignon Blanc

Flaunt Your Fillet

Great approaches deserve a rich reward!

Fillet of Sole in Orange Sherry Sauce

Step One:

1 lb. petrale sole fillets
salt to taste
1 cup dry sherry

Preheat oven to 400°F. In flameproof baking dish, place fillets in single layer and season with salt. Pour sherry over fillets and cover with foil. Bake 10-15 minutes, or until fillets are opaque. Transfer sole to warm au gratin dishes or plates; cover loosely and keep warm. Place baking dish over medium-high heat and reduce liquid to 2/3 cup.

Step Two:

2 Tbsp. butter
1/4 cup minced shallot
1/2 cup whipping cream
3 Tbsp. orange liqueur (curaçao, Grand Marnier)
grated orange peel from half an orange

Melt butter in frying pan over medium heat and sauté shallots until tender. Add fish liquid, cream, liqueur, and orange peel. Bring mixture to a boil; reduce heat and simmer 5 minutes. Nap fillets with sauce and serve immediately.

SUGGESTED MENU

"Fore" Play
Chive and Salmon Spread

Fast Greens
Walnut, Pear, and Blue Cheese Salad

Shoot to Thrill
Flaunt Your Fillet

It's a Gimme
Sautéed Mushrooms with Madeira and Pine Nuts

Wine
Riesling

♥ Scoring with Scallops

Mae West proved she knew the score when she said, "The score never interested me, only the game!"

Prawns and Scallops in Drambuie Butter Sauce

Step One:

1/2 lb. fresh ocean scallops
3/4 lb. medium prawns, shelled and
    deveined
3 Tbsp. butter
1/4 cup scotch
1/2 cup Drambuie

Melt butter in frying pan over medium heat. Add scallops and prawns, tossing to coat. Add scotch and Drambuie; warm for 15 seconds and ignite with a match. Turn heat to low and shake pan until flames disappear. Remove scallops and prawns to warm plate; cover loosely and keep warm.

Step Two:

1/4 cup bottled clam juice
1/3 cup fresh peas (or thawed frozen
    peas)
1/3 cup julienned carrots
1/3 cup julienned rutabaga

Whisk clam juice into pan; add vegetables and bring to a boil over medium-high heat. Boil until liquid is reduced by half, about 6 minutes.

Step Three:

3 Tbsp. butter
1 Tbsp. fresh lemon juice
salt and pepper to taste
1 1/2 cups fresh spinach leaves,
    washed, stems removed

Adjust heat to medium-low and add butter to pan 1 tablespoon at a time, whisking until melted. Add lemon juice and seasonings. Add prawns, scallops, and spinach. Cook until spinach is just wilted. Serve in warmed au gratins or on plates.

SCORE CARD

SUGGESTED MENU

1

2
"Fore" Play
Hot Crab Morsels

3
Fast Greens

4
Orange, Avocado, and

Pine Nut Salad
5

Shoot to Thrill
6
♥ *Scoring with Scallops*

7

It's a Gimme
8
French Kissed Peas

9
Wine

Chenin Blanc

♥ Match Play

It really is how *you play the game that counts!*

Shrimp in Tequila Butter Sauce with Rice

Step One:

1 jalapeño pepper, seeded, minced
1/4 cup tequila
1/4 cup fresh lime juice
2 Tbsp. brown sugar
1/8 tsp. cumin
1/4 cup light oil
3 cloves garlic, minced
1 lb. shrimp, shelled, deveined, and
    butterflied

Reserve 1 tsp. minced jalapeño for Step Three. Put remainder of pepper in a bowl; add tequila, lime, sugar, cumin, oil, and garlic. Stir until well blended. Add shrimp and marinate for 1 hour.

Step Two:

1 1/2 cups rice

Cook rice according to package directions. While rice is cooking, start Step Three.

Step Three:

2 Tbsp. butter
1/4 cup tequila
1 tsp. minced jalapeño pepper
1 clove garlic, minced
3 Tbsp. chopped fresh cilantro
2 Tbsp. chilled butter

Drain shrimp, reserve marinade. Melt butter in frying pan over high heat. Add shrimp and sauté 1 minute, until pink. Move shrimp to bowl. Add half of the marinade to pan and continue cooking over high heat until reduced by half. Add tequila, reserved jalapeño, garlic, cilantro, and chilled butter and whisk until blended. Ignite mixture with kitchen match and swirl slowly until flame dies. Spoon rice onto warmed plates. Arrange shrimp over rice and ladle sauce over shrimp and rice. Garnish with cilantro sprigs.

"Fore" Play

Corn, Basil, and Sun-Dried Tomato Cakes

Fast Greens

Orange, Avocado, and Pine Nut Salad

Shoot to Thrill

♥*Match Play*

It's a Gimme

French Kissed Peas

Wine

Sauvignon Blanc

Bogey Kabobs

2 hours

A kiss is just a kiss . . . unless you're way over par!

Scallop and Prawn Kabobs

Step One:

1/2 cup light soy sauce
2 Tbsp. sesame oil
2 Tbsp. dry sherry
1 Tbsp. minced fresh ginger
1 clove garlic, minced
6 large mushrooms, Crimini or white, quartered
2 thin zucchini, sliced 1/2" thick
1/2 basket cherry tomatoes
1/2 lb. large prawns, shelled and butterflied
1/2 lb. sea bass, cut into cubes
1/2 lb. sea scallops

Combine all ingredients except vegetables and seafood in large baking dish. Blend well. Add seafood and vegetables, turning to coat. Marinate for 1 hour at room temperature.

Step Two:

3 Tbsp. butter
1 clove garlic, minced
2 Tbsp. dry white wine
1 tsp. dry cilantro
1/8 tsp. cayenne pepper

In small saucepan, sauté garlic in butter until soft. Add remaining ingredients. Whisk until well blended. Set aside.

Step Three:

Turn grill to medium-high. Skewer and grill zucchini and mushrooms first. Brush with garlic butter and cook, turning frequently, until done. Keep warm in oven. Repeat with prawns and sea bass and finally with scallops and tomatoes, which cook fastest. Brush with remaining garlic butter and serve immediately on warm plates.

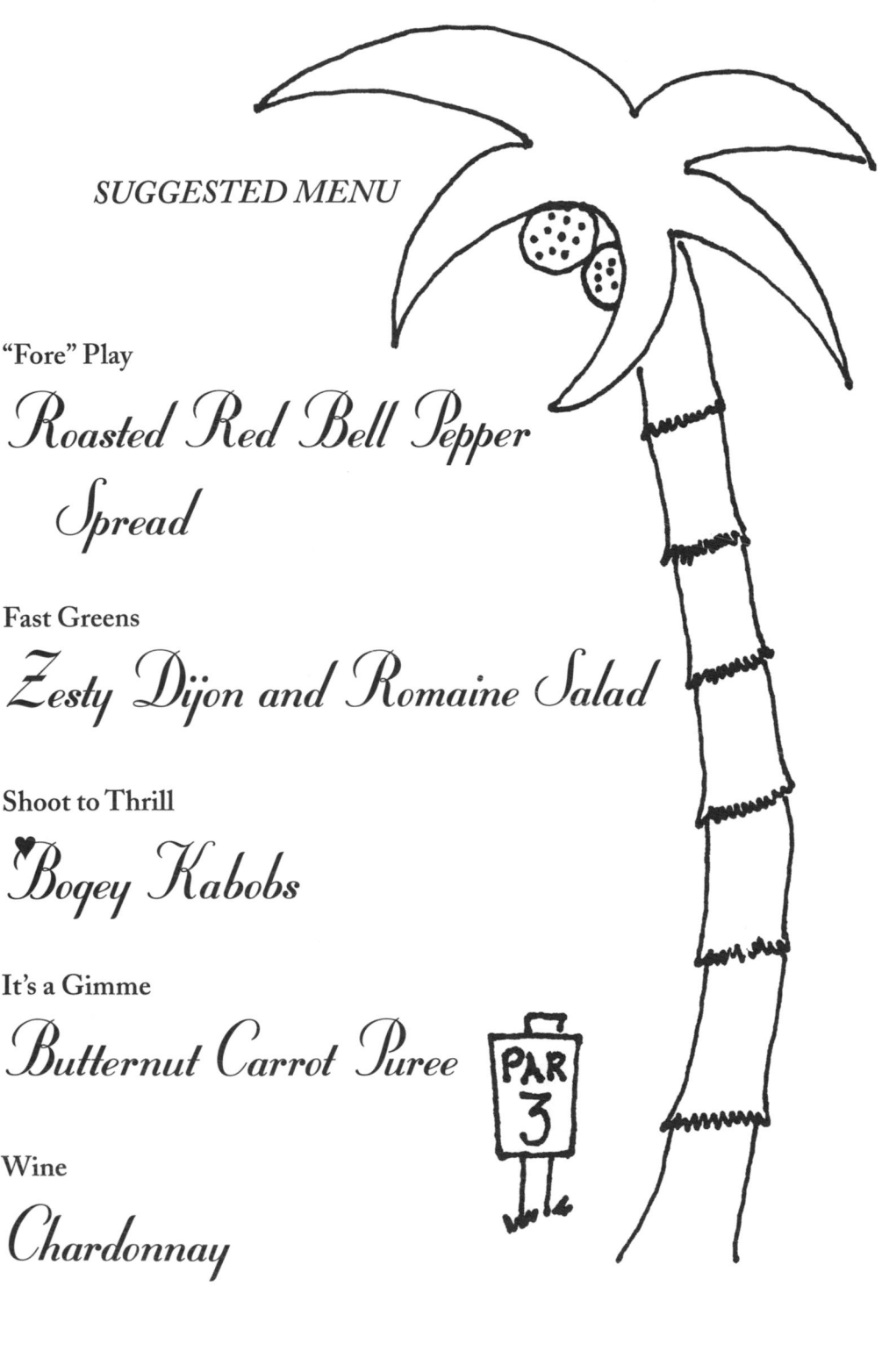

SUGGESTED MENU

"Fore" Play

Roasted Red Bell Pepper Spread

Fast Greens

Zesty Dijon and Romaine Salad

Shoot to Thrill

♥Bogey Kabobs

It's a Gimme

Butternut Carrot Puree

Wine

Chardonnay

# A Hole in One

. . . makes you the hottest driver on the course . . . any course!

Salmon Fillets in Mushroom Tomato Sauce

Step One:

2 Tbsp. butter
1 small onion, minced
8-10 mushrooms, chopped
4 tomatoes, peeled and chopped
1/2 cup dry white wine
1 Tbsp. tomato paste
1/2 cup Madeira
3/4 cup whipping cream
1 Tbsp. minced fresh parsley

Melt butter in frying pan over medium heat. Add onion and mushrooms; sauté until soft. Add tomatoes, wine, and tomato paste. Whisk constantly until no liquid remains. Add Madeira and again whisk until liquid has evaporated. Add cream; whisk until thickened. Stir in parsley.

Step Two:

2 Tbsp. butter
1 lb. salmon fillets
lemon wedges
parsley sprigs

Melt butter in large frying pan over high heat. Add salmon and sauté until just opaque. Lay fillets on warm plates and nap with sauce. Garnish with lemons and parsley. Serve.

SUGGESTED MENU

"Fore" Play

Roasted Red Bell Pepper Spread

Fast Greens

Walnut, Pear, and Blue Cheese Salad

Shoot to Thrill

A Hole in One

It's a Gimme

Sautéed Mushrooms with Madeira and Pine Nuts

Wine

Chardonnay

♥ Let's Swing

You're 'driving' me crazy!

White Bean and Mussel Salad

Step One:

1 1/2 to 2 lb. mussels, scrubbed and debearded

Soak mussels in large bowl of cold water for 10 minutes or more.

Step Two:

2 Tbsp. butter
1 small onion, minced
1/2 cup dry white wine

Melt butter in saucepan. Sauté onion until softened. Add wine, bring to a boil. Add mussels; cover and steam 4-5 minutes, until open. Discard any that do not open. Move mussels to bowl with slotted spoon. Boil cooking liquid until reduced by half.

Step Three:

1/4 cup olive oil
1/2 tsp. Dijon mustard
2 Tbsp. sherry wine vinegar
1/4 tsp. freshly ground pepper
salt to taste
1/4 cup minced parsley
2 15-oz. cans small white beans, drained and rinsed
1/2 lb. mixed greens (e.g., arugula, radicchio, butter leaf, red leaf, romaine)

In second small bowl, whisk 1/2 cup cooking liquid with oil, mustard, vinegar, salt, pepper, and parsley. Remove mussels from their shells and add to mix. Add white beans and gently toss to coat with dressing. Arrange a bed of mixed greens on plates, top with mussel and bean salad, and serve with crusty French bread.

SUGGESTED MENU

"Fore" Play

Chive and Salmon Spread

Shoot to Thrill

♥Let's Swing

It's a Gimme

Swiss Cauliflower

Wine

Chardonnay

I'm Trapped by Your Love
You're my only real hazard!

45 minutes

Robust Crab and Tomato Sauce with Spaghettini

Step One:

1 Tbsp. butter
1 clove garlic, minced
1/2 cup chopped green onions
3-4 Roma tomatoes, chopped
1/4 cup chicken broth

Melt butter in frying pan; sauté garlic and onion until soft. Add tomatoes and chicken broth, turn heat to medium and bring to a boil. Reduce heat and simmer 2 minutes.

Step Two:

1 cooked crab, cleaned and meat
   removed
1 Tbsp. fresh lemon juice
1/2 tsp. celery salt
1/4 cup chopped fresh parsley

Gently stir in crabmeat, lemon juice, and seasonings. Simmer 2 additional minutes.

Step Three:

1/2 lb. spaghettini
1/4 cup chopped parsley

Cook spaghettini according to package directions; drain. Mound pasta onto warm plates. Ladle sauce over pasta and sprinkle with parsley.

SUGGESTED MENU

"Fore" Play
Feta Cheese Spread

Fast Greens
Zesty Dijon and Romaine Salad

Shoot to Thrill
♥I'm Trapped by Your Love

It's a Gimme
*Green Beans with Prosciutto
and Parmesan*

Wine
Merlot

# Hooking Ewe

. . . was the best thing I ever did!

Lamb with Cinnamon, Almonds, and Raisins

Step One:
1 1/2 lb. lamb breast or shoulder, cut
    into bite-size cubes
salt and pepper to taste
2 Tbsp. butter
1 medium onion, minced
1/2 cup beef broth
1/4 tsp. ground saffron
1 small cinnamon stick

Season lamb with salt and pepper. Melt butter in frying pan over medium-high heat. Sauté onion and lamb until onion is tender and lamb is browned. Heat broth in small pan; add saffron and stir to dissolve. Blend broth into lamb. Add cinnamon. Reduce heat to low and simmer 1 1/2 hours.

Step Two:
1/2 cup blanched whole almonds

Meanwhile, place almonds in single layer in pie pan and toast in oven at 350°F until lightly browned, about 10 minutes. Stir occasionally.

Step Three:
1 Tbsp. honey
1/8 tsp. cinnamon
1/2 cup raisins

Move lamb to bowl with slotted spoon. Discard cinnamon stick. Add honey and cinnamon to frying pan and simmer 5 minutes. Return lamb to pan. Add raisins and simmer 5 minutes.

Step Four:
toasted almonds
sesame seeds

Spoon lamb onto warmed plates or au gratins; sprinkle with almonds and sesame seeds.

"Fore" Play

Feta Cheese Spread

Fast Greens

Orange, Avocado, and Pine Nut Salad

Shoot to Thrill

Hooking Ewe

It's a Gimme

French Kissed Peas

Wine

Merlot

Are Ewe Game?

I should warn you—I'm keeping score, and winner takes all!

Lamb Chops with Rosemary Burgundy Baste

Step One:

2 lamb sirloin chops, 1" thick
2 cloves garlic, peeled and halved

Rub lamb on all sides with garlic.

Step Two:

1 Tbsp. butter
1 1/2 tsp. fresh rosemary, bruised
1/2 cup burgundy

Melt butter in small saucepan over medium heat. Add rosemary and cook 1 minute. Blend in wine.

Step Three:

salt and pepper to taste
fresh rosemary sprigs

Season chops. Brush with wine-and-herb basting sauce. Grill or broil chops over high flame 4-7 minutes per side, basting frequently. Garnish with fresh rosemary sprigs and serve.

SUGGESTED MENU

"Fore" Play
Feta Cheese Spread

Fast Greens
Zesty Dijon and Romaine Salad

Shoot to Thrill
Are Ewe Game

It's a Gimme
Red Potatoes with Chive and Pepper Butter

Wine
Cabernet Sauvignon

♥ *Lovers' Folly*

Don't dillydally with the tally!

Penne Pasta with Sun-Dried Tomatoes, Fresh Basil, and Kalamata Olives

Step One:

1/4 cup loosely packed basil leaves
1/4 cup sun-dried tomatoes, in oil
2 Tbsp. balsamic vinegar
1/3 cup light olive oil
salt to taste
freshly ground pepper to taste

Chop basil leaves and tomatoes and place in bowl. Add vinegar. Whisk in oil, salt, and pepper until well blended.

Step Two:

1 red bell pepper, halved and seeded

Roast pepper over flame or under broiler until charred. Place in paper bag and fold top tightly; steam 10 minutes. Remove, scrape off charred parts, and chop coursely.

Step Three:

2 large portabello mushrooms, stems removed

Preheat grill. Brush mushrooms with tomato-basil dressing and grill until tender. Remove and slice into 1/4" strips.

Step Four:

3/4 lb. penne pasta
1/2 cup chopped Kalamata olives
1 cup canned garbanzo beans, drained

Cook pasta according to package directions; drain. Pour into bowl. Add olives, beans, peppers, and mushrooms. Toss with tomato-basil mixture.

Step Five:

1/2 cup crumbled feta cheese

Mound pasta on warm plate. Sprinkle with feta cheese and serve.

SUGGESTED MENU

"Fore" Play

Feta Cheese Spread

Fast Greens

Zesty Dijon and Romaine Salad

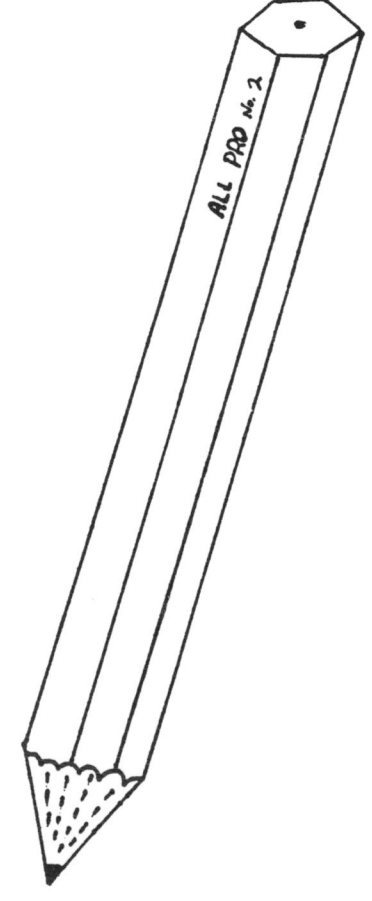

Shoot to Thrill

♥ *Lovers' Folly*

It's a Gimme

Swiss Cauliflower

Wine

Zinfandel

Fairway 'Fore' Play

All's fair in love and golf!

1 hour, 45 minutes

Gratin of White Beans, Pesto, and Pasta

Step One:

1 Tbsp. olive oil
1/2 onion, finely chopped
1 bay leaf
1/2 tsp. thyme
1 can small white beans, drained
and rinsed
1 cup water

Heat oil in saucepan and sauté onion until soft. Add remaining ingredients and cook on low 5 minutes.

Step Two:

3 cloves garlic, coursely chopped
2 cups parsley, coursely chopped
1/4 cup olive oil
1 1/4 cups grated Asiago or Parmesan
cheese
1/4 tsp. salt
1/2 tsp. freshly ground pepper

Preheat oven to 350°F. In food processor, pulse garlic and parsley until well blended. With machine running, add oil in thin stream. Scrape down sides. Add cheese, salt, and pepper. Process to a course puree.

Step Three:

2 cups uncooked small pasta, such as
bowtie
3-4 large Roma tomatoes, chopped
salt and pepper to taste
3/4 cup small curd cottage cheese
1 Tbsp. olive oil
2/3 cup dry seasoned bread crumbs

Cook pasta according to package directions, until al dente. Drain. To medium bowl, add pasta, beans and broth, parsley sauce, and tomatoes. Add salt and pepper; mix well. Turn into a baking dish. Drop tablespoons of cottage cheese on top of pasta and push them beneath the surface. Mix oil and bread crumbs. Sprinkle over top. Bake 35 minutes.

SUGGESTED MENU

"Fore" Play
Feta Cheese Spread

Fast Greens
Orange, Avocado, and Pine Nut Salad

Shoot to Thrill
Fairway 'Fore' Play

It's a Gimme
Butternut Carrot Puree

Wine
Pinot Grigio

A Passionate Puzzle

40 minutes

To paraphrase Gary Player, "Golf, like love, is a puzzle without an answer."

Smoky Prosciutto, Roasted Red Pepper, and Pine Nut Pizza

Step One:

2 Tbsp. light olive oil
1 medium-size red onion, finely
   chopped
3 cloves garlic, minced
3/4 cup chopped Crimini mushrooms
4 Roma tomatoes, finely chopped
1/4 cup chopped fresh basil
2 Tbsp. chopped parsley

Preheat oven to 450°F. In frying pan over medium heat, sauté onions until soft. Add garlic and mushrooms and sauté until mushrooms are tender. Add remaining ingredients and simmer 10-15 minutes.

Step Two:

1/4 cup pine nuts

Toast pine nuts in dry frying pan over medium heat until golden brown.

Step Three:

1/2 red bell pepper

Roast pepper over flame or under broiler until charred. Place in paper bag and fold top tightly; steam 10 minutes. Remove charred portion and chop.

Step Four:

1 Boboli or other prepared crust
1 cup shredded mozzarella cheese
3 paper-thin slices prosciutto, chopped
1/4 cup Asiago or Parmesan cheese

Place pizza crust on pizza pan and top with tomato sauce. Spread mozzarella evenly over sauce. Sprinkle peppers, prosciutto, and pine nuts over pizza. Top with Asiago or Parmesan cheese. Bake 10 minutes.

SUGGESTED MENU

"Fore" Play

Roasted Red Bell Pepper Spread

Fast Greens

Zesty Dijon and Romaine Salad

Shoot to Thrill

A Passionate Puzzle

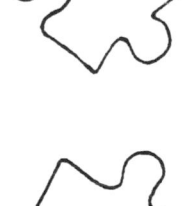

It's a Gimme

Green Beans with Prosciutto and Parmesan

Wine

Pinot Noir

♥My Preferred Lie

... would be lying in wait for you!

1 hour, 45 minutes

Pork, Sweet Potato, and Cranberry Salad

Step One:

5 Tbsp. bourbon
5 Tbsp. Dijon mustard
6 Tbsp. molasses
1/4 tsp. hot pepper sauce
4 pork loin chops, 1" thick, trimmed
   of fat
2 sweet potatoes, peeled and cut into
   1/4" slices

Combine bourbon, mustard, hot pepper sauce, and molasses; blend well. Divide into 2 bowls. Lay pork chops and sweet potato slices on cookie sheet in single layer. Brush with marinade, reserving leftover. Set aside at room temperature for 30-45 minutes.

Step Two:

Preheat grill or broiler. Grill or broil chops 4" from heat for about 6 minutes; turn and continue another 4-6 minutes or until white and moist inside and browned on outside. Move to plate. Grill sweet potato slices 6-7 minutes on each side, until soft.

Step Three:

1/4 cup lime juice
3 Tbsp. minced fresh chives
1 Tbsp. minced fresh parsley
3/4 tsp. salt
1/2 tsp. freshly ground pepper
1/2 cup light olive oil
1/3 cup cranberries

In medium bowl, combine 3 Tbsp. reserved marinade with remaining ingredients except cranberries, whisking until well blended. Cut pork into bite-size cubes; move to clean bowl. Add sweet potatoes and cranberries. Add a little dressing and toss gently to coat.

Step Four:

1/2 lb. mixed greens (e.g., spinach,
   romaine, arugula, radicchio, butter
   leaf, etc.)

Divide greens onto plates. Drizzle with dressing. Arrange pork, sweet potatoes, and cranberries on top of greens.

SUGGESTED MENU

"Fore" Play

Hot Crab Morsels

Shoot to Thrill

♥My Preferred Lie

It's a Gimme

Sautéed Mushrooms with Madeira and Pine Nuts

Wine

Gamay Beaujolais

♥*In the Rough*

. . . and ready for action!

Orange Glazed Pork Ribs

Step One:

3 onions, quartered
4 cloves garlic, split
1 Tbsp. salt
1-2 lb. pork back ribs

Fill large stock pot with water. Add onion, garlic, and salt. Bring to a boil. Add ribs; simmer 25 minutes.

Step Two:

1/2 cup sugar
1/2 cup apple cider vinegar
4 cloves garlic, minced
2 Tbsp. frozen orange juice
   concentrate
1 orange peel, grated
3/4 tsp. dry mustard
1 1/2 Tbsp. minced fresh ginger
1/4 cup bourbon

Combine all ingredients except bourbon in small saucepan. Turn heat to low and simmer 5 minutes. Add bourbon; simmer 3 minutes. Drain ribs and place in container just large enough to hold them. Pour glaze over ribs and cover; refrigerate overnight.

Step Three:

1 orange, sliced

Line baking pan with foil. Place ribs, curved side down, in pan. Brush with glaze. Bake at 400°F for 25 minutes. Turn ribs and brush with glaze; bake 10 minutes more. Move ribs to serving platter and garnish with orange slices.

SUGGESTED MENU

"Fore" Play
Roasted Red Bell Pepper Spread

Fast Greens
Zesty Dijon and Romaine Salad

Shoot to Thrill
♥In the Rough

It's a Gimme
Butternut Carrot Puree

Wine
Gamay Beaujolais

 *Hooked on You*

. . . no matter how you slice it!

Pork Fillets in Zinfandel Herb Sauce

Step One:

2 Tbsp. flour
2 large pork loin fillets, boned
2 Tbsp. olive oil

Place flour and pork in plastic bag and shake to coat. Pour oil into frying pan and brown chops over medium heat until golden brown.

Step Two:

5 green onions, chopped
1 carrot, chopped
1 tsp. marjoram
1/2 tsp. thyme
1/2 tsp. oregano
1 bay leaf
1 cup chicken broth
1 cup Zinfandel

Add vegetables and herbs to frying pan and sauté over medium heat until tender, about 20 minutes. Add stock and wine; cover and cook over low heat 40 minutes.

Step Three:

20 cloves garlic, peeled

Heat oven to 350°F. Strain vegetables from sauce and discard. Add garlic; cover and bake 1 hour.

Step Four:

2 Tbsp. minced orange peel
4 Tbsp. butter
1/2 lb. egg noodles, cooked
1 Tbsp. minced orange peel

Transfer pork to au gratin dishes. Add orange peel to sauce. Whisk butter into sauce, 1 Tbsp. at a time. Arrange noodles next to pork and nap pork with sauce. Sprinkle with orange and serve.

"Fore" Play

Crab Caps

Fast Greens

Zesty Dijon and Romaine Salad

Shoot to Thrill

Hooked on You

It's a Gimme

Sautéed Mushrooms with Madeira and Pine Nuts

Wine

Zinfandel

♥ Love Conquers All

But "no one ever conquers golf!" So said Kathy Whitworth.

Summer Cold Cut Salad

Step One:

1 2-oz. can anchovy fillets, drained
2 Tbsp. chopped parsley
1/2 onion, quartered
3 cloves garlic, sliced
1/3 cup cold water
2 Tbsp. lemon juice
1/4 tsp. tarragon
1/4 tsp. marjoram
3/4 cup light olive oil

Using a blender or food processor, puree all ingredients except olive oil. With appliance running, add olive oil in a slow steady stream until dressing thickens.

Step Two:

1/2 lb. mixed greens (e.g., romaine, butter leaf, red leaf)
1/4 lb. sliced roast beef
1/4 lb. sliced ham
1/4 lb. sliced turkey
1/2 red bell pepper, thinly sliced
1/2 cucumber, peeled and sliced
10 cherry tomatoes, halved
8 white mushrooms, sliced
1/3 cup pitted black olives

Divide mixed greens onto chilled plates. Arrange meats and vegetables on greens and drizzle dressing over top. Serve with crusty French bread.

SUGGESTED MENU

"Fore" Play

Corn, Basil, and Sun-Dried Tomato Cakes

Shoot to Thrill

♥ Love Conquers All

It's a Gimme

Red Potatoes with Chive and Pepper Butter

Wine

Zinfandel

Swiss Cauliflower

25 minutes

Step One:

1 small head cauliflower, broken into
    florets
1 tsp. salt

Bring pot of salted water to boil. Add cauliflower and cook, covered, 8-10 minutes. Remove and drain. Place in greased casseroles.

Step Two:

1/2 cup grated Swiss cheese
1/3 cup freshly grated Parmesan cheese
1/4 cup seasoned bread crumbs
2 Tbsp. butter

Preheat oven to 400°F. In a bowl, combine cheese, bread crumbs, and butter. Sprinkle over cauliflower. Bake until cheeses bubble and begin to brown, about 10 minutes.

Butternut Carrot Puree

30 minutes

Step One:

1/2 butternut squash
3 carrots, peeled and cut into 2" pieces

Peel squash and cut into 2" chunks. Steam until tender, about 15 minutes. Place in food processor. Steam carrots until tender and add to food processor.

Step Two:

2 tsp. sherry
1 1/2 tsp. brown sugar
1/8 tsp. mace
1/8 tsp. ground coriander
pinch nutmeg
freshly ground pepper
3 Tbsp. butter
paprika, for garnish

Add sherry, brown sugar, and spices to food processor and blend. Add butter and blend until light and fluffy. Garnish with a sprinkle of paprika.

Sautéed Mushrooms with Madeira and Pine Nuts

30 minutes

Step One:

1/2 cup finely chopped prosciutto
1 Tbsp. light olive oil
1/4 cup pine nuts

Heat oil in frying pan over low heat; lightly brown prosciutto. Move to small bowl. Add pine nuts to pan and increase heat to medium. Sauté until golden; add to ham in bowl.

Step Two:

1 Tbsp. light olive oil
1 clove garlic, minced
1 shallot, minced
1/2 lb. mushrooms, sliced
3 large mushrooms, minced

Reduce heat to low, adding oil if needed. Sauté garlic and shallot until tender. Increase heat to medium-high. Add mushrooms and sauté, stirring frequently, until mushrooms just begin to lose their juices.

Step Three:

2 Tbsp. Madeira
2 Tbsp. whipping cream
2 Tbsp. minced parsley

Add Madeira and boil until liquid is reduced to 2 Tbsp. Add cream; reduce heat to low and cook until sauce thickens. Stir in parsley, ham, and pine nuts. Serve immediately.

Green Beans with Prosciutto and Parmesan

30 minutes

Step One:

1/3 lb. green beans

Steam or boil green beans until crisp-tender.

Step Two:

1 Tbsp. butter
2 Tbsp. pine nuts
1 clove garlic, minced
2 Tbsp. diced prosciutto or other lean ham
2 Tbsp. grated Parmesan cheese

Melt butter in frying pan over medium heat. Add pine nuts and sauté until golden brown. Add garlic, green beans, and prosciutto; sauté 3-4 minutes. Toss with Parmesan. Serve.

Red Potatoes with Chive and Pepper Butter

35 minutes

Step One:

1/2 small red bell pepper
1/2 small green bell pepper

Seed and rinse peppers; roast until charred over open flame or under broiler. Place in paper bag and fold top tightly. Steam 10 minutes. Scrape and discard charred skin from peppers; chop finely.

Step Two:

6-8 small red potatoes, quartered

Steam potatoes until done, 10-15 minutes.

Step Three:

2 Tbsp. butter
2 Tbsp. minced fresh chives
salt to taste
freshly ground pepper to taste

Melt butter in frying pan over medium heat. Add peppers and sauté 2-3 minutes. Add potatoes and chives. Season with salt and pepper and toss gently.

French Kissed Peas

15 minutes

2 Tbsp. butter
3/4 cup chopped lettuce
1 1/2 cups fresh peas or frozen petite peas
2 Tbsp. minced shallot
1 tsp. minced fresh parsley
3/4 Tbsp. sugar
salt and pepper to taste

Melt butter in large saucepan. Place lettuce on top of butter. Add remaining ingredients and simmer 10 minutes, stirring occasionally.

SUBJECT INDEX

RECIPE INDEX

SCORECARD
(Notes)

SCORECARD
(Notes)

SCORECARD
(Notes)

SCORECARD
(Notes)

SCORECARD
(Notes)

96